THIRTY DAYS TO BECOMING A DISCIPLE-MAKING LEADER

KEN ADAMS

Thirty Days to Becoming a Disciple-Making Leader
impactdisciples.com

Copyright ©2024 by Ken Adams

Scripture quotations are from the ESV® Bible (The Holy Bible, English Standard Version®), copyright © 2001 by Crossway, a publishing ministry of Good News Publishers. Used by permission. All rights reserved.

All rights reserved. No part of this publication may be reproduced, stored in a retrieval system, or transmitted in any form or by any means - electronic, mechanical, photocopy, recording, or any other - except for brief quotations in printed reviews, without prior permission of the publisher.

Written by Ken Adams
Designed by Grace Asnip

BEFORE YOU BEGIN...

Let me start with a confession. I have never been discipled, at least not in the formal sense. I have been part of a church for over sixty years, a Christian for over fifty-five years, and a Pastor for over thirty years. I have yet to be discipled by someone in a discipleship group that meets weekly to study God's Word, hold each other accountable, support each other, and pray for each other. Like far too many Christians, I grew up in a church where disciple-making and discipleship were not the focus. So, I was never invited to participate in a discipleship group.

Formal discipleship has never happened for me, but informal discipleship has. I have had countless numbers of people invest in my life and help me learn how to follow Jesus. I am grateful that God has seen fit to help me become a fully trained disciple, even if it did not happen intentionally. Unintentional disciple-making is better than no disciple-making!

As a pastor, I have learned the importance of disciple-making and discipleship. After decades of leading a church to become a disciple-making movement, I have learned how to lead discipleship groups and have led more groups than I can count. Through the school of head knocks, Scripture, and the Holy Spirit, I have learned some of the critical priorities of being a disciple-making leader.

In this book, I will share what I have learned and what scripture teaches about being a disciple-making leader. You won't become a disciple-making leader in thirty days, but you can gain an understanding of some of the key concepts and priorities that we see in God's Word.

You do not need to be an ordained minister or have a seminary degree to make disciples. You need to be a disciple that demonstrates you are growing in the character and conduct of Christ. That's all Jesus' disciples had when he commissioned them to "make disciples of all nations."

Over the next few weeks, you will discover some, not all, of the principles necessary to be an excellent disciple-making leader. I pray that this short book will encourage, inspire, and help you become the leader God wants you to be.

Being and Building Disciples,

Ken Adams

DAY ONE

"Leaders Needed"

The Church desperately needs leaders, but not just any kind of leaders. The Church needs disciple-making leaders; leaders who understand the its mission is to "make disciples of all nations."

A church without disciple-making leaders is like a baseball team with a coach who has never played baseball. It is like an army with officers who have never shot a gun. It is like a university with teachers who have never been to school. It is like a business with a manager who has never used their service or product. When you think about it, it is absurd to think the Church is being led to make disciples of all nations with leaders who have never been discipled or made disciples. That includes most pastors.

It is doubtful that a person will lead toward a mission they don't know or have never experienced, which is the problem in the Church today. We have churches worldwide filled with leaders who are clueless about what they should be leading the church to accomplish. If church leaders do not know that the mission is to make disciples of all nations, we shouldn't be surprised if that isn't happening. Yes, the Church needs leaders, but we need the right leaders. The Church desperately needs disciple-making leaders.

When the Church is led by pastors and leaders who understand and live out the mission of the Church, great things happen. People are reached. Lives are changed. God is glorified. This is precisely what we see in Acts. When the Church was born in Jerusalem, it was led by disciple-making leaders. The apostles had been Christ's disciples and were committed to developing and appointing more disciple-making leaders. The results were fantastic. Hundreds of thousands came to know Christ in the first few decades of the church. Tens of thousands went from being untrained seekers to fully trained disciples. God's glory was being spread from Jerusalem to Judaea and Samaria and the ends of the earth.

What happened in Acts can happen again today. We need the Church to get back to developing disciple-making leaders. In the pages of this small resource, you will discover some of the priorities of what a disciple-making leader looks like. Disciple-making leaders are the kind of leaders the Church needs.

DIG DEEPER

Please read **John 20:21** and write one insight you gleaned from it.

_____
_____
_____

DAY TWO

"The Greatest Leader Ever"

The most outstanding leader to ever live is Jesus. He is also a disciple-making leader. He created the most significant and most extensive movement in the history of humanity. That movement is called Christianity. It has changed the world and remains the most critical movement ever.

Jesus created this movement by making disciples that would make disciples. He started by making his disciples and then appointed fully trained disciples to be leaders. The apostles were the very first generation of disciple-making leaders in the church of Jesus Christ. The movement they began in Jerusalem spread to all nations.

Jesus modeled three things for his disciples. He modeled for them the right heart, knowledge, and understanding needed to lead a disciple-making movement. They learned firsthand what it meant to be a leader after God's heart. They learned up close and personal what they needed to know to lead like Jesus. They gained the understanding needed to teach others and to pass on to others what had been passed on to them.

It is pronounced that Jesus' movement needed leaders but required disciple-making leaders. Jesus didn't build his movement with business, educational, military, political, or athletic team leaders. He made his leaders out of the disciples that he had trained. Jesus knew that disciple-making leaders come out of discipleship environments. Jesus developed his leaders the same way the church needs to develop leaders today.

When a church is committed to making fully trained disciples, it builds a pool of potentially qualified leaders from whom to choose. The church making fully trained disciples will always have plenty of potential leaders.

Jesus didn't just build leaders; he made disciple-making leaders who knew how to lead others the way they had been taught. In the upcoming daily lessons, you will discover some of the priorities of great disciple-making leaders.

DIG DEEPER

Please read **Jeremiah 3:15** and write one insight you gleaned from it.

_____
_____
_____

DAY THREE

"Mission Requires Leadership"

Several years ago, I ran across the verse, Jeremiah 3:15, that helped me understand and define the type of leadership needed in the Church today. You need to read the entire chapter when you have time, but notice specifically that God says to his people, "Then I will give you shepherds after my own heart, who will lead you with knowledge and understanding." (NIV)

This passage tells us that leadership is God's plan to return his people to himself. It is not a building, a board, a program, or a book. It is the right kind of leader. In Jeremiah's day, God planned to use leaders to lead his people away from false gods and idols and back to himself. Today is no different. God's plan to bring people back to himself in today's world is still leadership.

Remember that after the days of Jeremiah, God's people ended up in exile for a season before returning to their homes. Soon after their return to Jerusalem, God ceased to speak to his people. Then, after four hundred years of silence, God sends another leader. He sends a shepherd after God's heart with the knowledge and understanding to lead. That leader's name was Jesus! Jesus came to lead lost people back to God.

Over three years, Jesus developed leaders who would carry on his mission once he was gone. He wanted them to have a heart after God and the knowledge and understanding to lead. He wanted his disciple-making team to be leaders of Jeremiah 3:15.

We need leaders today with the same traits in Jeremiah 3:15. We observe those traits in Jesus, his apostles, and the apostles' disciples. We need a church filled with leaders with a heart for

God and the knowledge and understanding to lead the Church to become a movement of multiplying disciples.

A church filled with leaders who have the heart to be and build disciples who know how to live, lead, and leverage their influence like Jesus and understand how to share the mission, strategy, and passion with others is the kind of church the world needs today. Let's look a little deeper at the concept of a 315 Leader.

DIG DEEPER

Please read **Jeremiah 3:15** and write one insight you gleaned from it.

_____
_____
_____

DAY FOUR

"A Leader with a Heart After God"

Every church needs to be led by leaders with a heart after God. The heart is the key to extraordinary leadership, and leaders with the right heart will always move in the right direction. We know the truth of that statement from the books of Kings and Chronicles.

To be clear, having the right heart has nothing to do with the organ inside your chest, but it has everything to do with having a heart that is motivated, driven, and passionate about the same things God's heart is inspired, driven, and passionate about. When you tell a child, "Your heart is not in it," you speak to their motivation level. When you tell a child to "do it with all your heart," you are talking about their desire, not a muscle inside their chest.

When we talk about God's heart, we ask what motivated Jesus to do what he did. What drove him to leave heaven's glory, majesty, and splendor and come to a slimy, stinky, sorry place like Earth to do what he did? Jesus did what he did because he had a heart to see every person, nation, and generation know what it means to be a disciple and understand what it means to build more disciples. The Great Commandments and Great Commission drove Jesus to do what he did. Jesus was passionate about making disciples of all nations!

A leader with a heart after God is a leader who is driven by the same things that caused Jesus to do what he did. A leader with a heart after God is a leader with a significant commitment to the Great Commandment and the Great Commission. A leader with a heart after God is a leader who is passionate about being and building disciples of all nations.

Just imagine how different the Church would be if every leader were motivated, driven, and passionate about the same thing Jesus was inspired, driven, and passionate about. A church filled with leaders with hearts after God would be a mission-driven church. It would be a church where people learn what it means to be disciples and build more disciples. It would be the church exactly the way Jesus designed it to be. Remember, Jesus started the Church the way he wanted it; now he wants it the way he started it.

DIG DEEPER

Please read **Proverbs 4:23** and write one insight you gleaned from it.

_____
_____
_____

DAY FIVE

"A Leader with the Knowledge to Lead"

God wants his Church to be led by leaders who have a heart after him and leaders who have the knowledge to teach. So, what does a leader need to know to have the proper knowledge?

Every leader needs to know what Jesus wanted his leaders to know. He wanted them to understand how to live the life he lived. He wanted them to know how to lead others the way he taught and leverage their influence through others the way he did.

Jesus modeled for his disciples the life he wanted them to live by displaying his character and conduct. He modeled for his disciples the way he wanted them to lead others by the way he led them from untrained seekers to fully trained disciples. Jesus modeled for his disciples how to leverage their influence through others by how he multiplied more disciples through their influence.

I don't know a single pastor who wouldn't want a church filled with leaders who know how to lead the same way Jesus taught his disciples—a church filled with leaders growing in Christ-like character and conduct. Growing in leading others to live like Jesus and leveraging their influence through others is a church that is on fire! You can't go wrong with a church of leaders with a heart after God and the knowledge to lead.

The Church in Jerusalem was a church that was led by 315 Leaders who had a heart after God and the knowledge to teach as Jesus instructed. We know this because Jesus had just spent three years equipping his disciples, who became that church's leaders (apostles.) Jesus spent three years helping this group of people develop the right kind of heart. He spent three years showing them how to live, lead, and leverage like he did. They received a first-hand demonstration of a 315 Leader.

Jesus was developing the leaders of his movement by being with them and modeling for them what he wanted them to know. Jesus knew that more was always caught than taught!

DIG DEEPER

Please read **Mark 3:14** and write one insight you gleaned from it.

_____
_____
_____

DAY SIX

"A Leader with the Understanding to Lead"

If all Jesus had done was to give his leaders a heart after God and the knowledge to lead, it might not have been translated to anyone else. Jesus could have helped his disciples get a heart after God and taught them what they needed to know to lead, but they had to understand how to pass it on to others. This is how Jesus kept his mission going. He gave leaders the understanding needed to lead others as they had been taught.

Teaching leaders the proper understanding is like passing the baton in a relay race. It is helping create multiple generations of disciples. It is precisely what is needed to ignite a movement of multiplying disciples. The inability to understand how to lead others would have shut down any momentum that Jesus had begun with his disciples. Jesus had spent three years teaching his disciples what they needed to know; now, they needed to understand how to pass it on to others without Jesus being there.

The books of Matthew, Mark, Luke, and John guide us to what Jesus wanted his disciples to know. The gospels teach how to live as Jesus lived. Lead like Jesus led, and leverage your influence through others the way Jesus leveraged his. The book of Acts guides us to what he wanted his disciples to understand. Jesus wanted them to understand the importance of a shared mission, a shared strategy, and a shared passion.

The believers in Jerusalem all shared the same mission. They all knew the mission was to make disciples of all nations. There was no disagreement or confusion on the mission Jesus had given them. They also shared the same strategy. They all worked the same strategy Jesus had used with them. They were helping untrained seekers become fully developed disciples of Christ. They also shared the same passion. They all gave their lives for the sake of the mission. There is no more significant sign of love than to die for something you believe in. All of the apostles died for the cause of Christ.

You have great power with a shared mission, strategy, and passion. Like concentrated light or water, when it is united, it creates energy. Church leaders who have understanding lead the church to make a powerful impact on the world around them. We need leaders with understanding today!

DIG DEEPER

Please read **Acts 1:1-2** and write one insight you gleaned from it.

_____
_____
_____

DAY SEVEN

"Six Priorities of Disciple-Making Leaders"

Once a person becomes a leader after God's heart and has the knowledge and understanding to lead, they are ready to become a disciple-making leader. Having the right heart, proper knowledge, and correct understanding makes a person the kind of leader God uses. They now have the foundation needed to begin living out the true priorities of every genuine disciple-maker.

As you study the examples of disciple-making leaders in scripture, you discover several common priorities of great disciple-makers. These six priorities are not the only of disciple-makers but are undoubtedly true of all great disciple-making leaders. The rest of this booklet will be devoted to helping you understand and grow in each of these priorities. The goal is that you become a great disciple-making leader who lives out the biblical priorities of disciple-makers.

> *Great leaders know the mission.*
> *Great leaders model the mission.*
> *Great leaders execute the mission.*
> *Great leaders multiply the mission.*
> *Great leaders protect the mission.*
> *Great leaders finish the mission.*

After pastoring for nearly thirty-five years, I know this much. A leader with a heart after God who has the knowledge and understanding to lead is a leader who is evident in the church's mission. They live out the mission in their own life. They do the mission consistently. They help others learn how to live out the mission. They fight for the mission and fight against disunity when it occurs. They live out the mission and leave behind a disciple-making legacy.

All leaders are not the same. Some leaders don't even need to be in leadership. They have been asked to lead before having the proper foundation. Some leaders need to know the priorities of a great leader. The next several weeks will give you a few priorities you'll be working on for years. You can be a great disciple-making leader. You have to be trained and equipped to be one.

DIG DEEPER

Please read **Ephesians 5:1** and write one insight you gleaned from it.

_____
_____
_____

QUESTIONS FOR REFLECTION OR DISCUSSION

The past seven days have taught you what it means to be a Disciple-Making Leader. Please take a few minutes to reflect on the following questions or discuss them with others.

1- Explain the difference between a leader and a disciple-making leader.

2- How did discipleship relate to leadership for Jesus?

3- In what ways could Jesus have been considered a 315 leader?

4- How is the "heart" the key to outstanding leadership?

5- What did Jesus want his leaders to know to lead well?

6- How would you describe the difference between knowledge and understanding regarding leadership?

7- How would you evaluate yourself when being a disciple-making leader?

DAY EIGHT

"Great Leaders Know the Mission"

I am 100% certain of this. No coach has ever been considered excellent who didn't know the mission of football was to win a championship. No general has ever been considered superior if they didn't see the mission of their army was to have victory over the enemy. No CEO has ever been given the title of remarkable if they did not know the mission of their for-profit business was to make a profit. Outstanding leadership requires knowing the mission.

I hope you see the big idea here. Outstanding leadership in the church begins with a leader who knows the church's mission. A leader cannot give the church great leadership if they are not focused on its mission. So here is the million-dollar question: what is the mission of Christ's church?

If you don't know how to answer that question or want to check your answer, look up Matthew 28:19 to find the correct answer.

I remember the day I realized the church had a mission problem. I was teaching a seminary class with thirty-two potential church leaders in attendance. It was a "Discipleship in the Local Church" class, and I thought a pop quiz concerning the mission would be appropriate on the first day of class. I asked all thirty-two students to take a piece of paper and write down the one imperative in Matthew 28:19. I then went around the room and asked each student to share their answer. Here is what was unbelievable. Only two in a room of thirty-two potential leaders in the

Church of Jesus Christ knew that the imperative (command) in Matthew 28:19 was "to make disciples."

That, my friend, is a sad commentary on today's church of Jesus Christ.

The church's mission is not to go, baptize, teach, worship, feed the poor, or love people. The mission is to "make disciples," we do that by going, baptizing, teaching, worshipping, and loving. Clarity is essential! Jesus did not say, "Make great worshippers, scholars, or evangelists." He said, "Make disciples." Every church needs to be led by pastors and leaders who are clear on the mission and willing to obey it. As a friend of mine often says, "Christ's last command ought to be our priority."

DIG DEEPER

Please read **Matthew 28:19-20** and write one insight you gleaned from it.

_____
_____
_____

DAY NINE

"The Problem of Mission Drift"

I once heard a guy make this statement. If you went to ten typical churches within a ten-mile radius of each other on a weekend and asked a leader what the church's mission was, you'd get ten different answers. I couldn't agree more.

It is hard to fathom how far the church has drifted from the mission of Jesus. It is mind-blowing that the church is all over the map when it comes to clarity regarding the mission. How have we gotten so far away from the original mission Jesus gave us?

If a professional football or baseball team starts the season and only twenty-five percent of the team knows the mission is to win the title, it is safe to say that the team is in big trouble. Even more so if that twenty-five percent is valid only for the organization's leaders. You must have all the leaders of an organization unified on the mission.

When Jesus commanded to "make disciples" on a mountainside in Galilee, the disciples did not walk down that mountain asking what they would do now. They did not debate over what the mission would be. They did not hold a business meeting to vote on the church's mission statement. No! Those disciples walked down that mountain in Galilee knowing that their mission, should they accept it (I've watched too many movies), was about making disciples of every person, nation, and generation. While waiting for Jesus to return, they knew exactly what they should do. They did not suffer from mission drift.

If church leaders drift from the church's original mission, it will not result in God's preferred outcome for the church. The church might accomplish some "good things," but those good things could be the enemy of the "best things." We must not let the enemy convince us to accomplish a mission, regardless of how good it might be, that Jesus never asked us to perform.

When it is all said and done, church leaders will be asked how well they led the church to accomplish one thing- the Great Commission. We will not be asked how well we did at doing one hundred other good things that distracted us from the main thing.

DIG DEEPER

Please read **Matthew 25:21** and write one insight you gleaned from it.

_____
_____
_____

DAY TEN

"Every Pastor's Wish"

Every pastor I know wishes to have a church filled with "mission-minded" leaders. All pastors share this wish because it is amazing how many problems go away when many leaders are on a mission together. Being mission-minded does wonders for keeping a church unified. It helps a church stay focused. It defines why a church exists, and being mission-minded enables you to know what to say "yes" to and what to say "no" to. It has been said, "When you forget you're why, you will lose your way!"

The world is filled with businesses, teams, schools, families, churches, and even countries that have forgotten their way. They have lost their way because they lost sight of why they exist. They have drifted off the mission; they are lost and going nowhere. This is exactly what Satan wishes for! Satan desires to keep the church in mission drift and divide church leaders on why the church exists to begin with. If the enemy can confuse church leaders on the mission, the church cannot fully accomplish what it was created to do in the first place. Expect Satan to bring confusion.

Satan's goal is to create self-minded leaders rather than mission-minded leaders. A self-minded leader is a leader who puts anything they want ahead of what God wants for the church. Anytime a leader thinks they know what's better for the church than Christ does, that is a self-minded leader. Self-minded leaders always create trouble for pastors wishing to see the church accomplish the mission of Christ.

The best thing a pastor can do for the church is point the church toward its mission. When a pastor can get every leader moving in the right direction and the same direction, good things are about to happen. To get everyone's mission, the pastor must talk about the mission, model the mission, and direct the mission. The pastor must be passionate about the mission. A great church has a pastor and leaders who share a passion for a great mission!

In Exodus 1:10, the new king of Egypt said, "Come, let us deal shrewdly with them, lest they multiply...". Be aware that a church with disciple-making leaders makes the enemy mad. He will fight against you, but more significant is he that is in you than he that is in the world.

DIG DEEPER

Please read **Exodus 1:7** and write one insight you gleaned from it.

_____
_____
_____

DAY ELEVEN

"Be a Mission-Minded Leader"

Every leader has a choice to make. Will they choose to be a mission-minded leader or a self-minded leader? Your choice will determine so many things in your life and your church. Many good things will happen if you decide to be a mission-minded leader. You will be a part of a church on a mission and experience so much fulfillment and joy from seeing what God does. You will be fruitful, and God will be honored by your commitment.

The self-minded leader will usually be an obstacle to unity in the church and a hindrance to fulfilling the mission. They will not have joy in their hearts and experience strife and conflict rather than peace and harmony. You want to avoid standing before the Lord someday and telling him you hurt his mission rather than helping it go forward. You do not want to be remembered as someone who stood against God's mission to make disciples of all nations. Being a mission-minded leader only requires a few simple things. It requires agreement, and it involves alignment.

Agreement means you know the mission, learn how to accomplish it and stand behind it. Alignment, however, means that you find your role to help make it happen. Alignment means involvement. People say they believe in something, but their actions show otherwise. Alignment means your actions demonstrate that the church is on the proper mission.

If I agree the mission is to make disciples, but I don't participate in a disciple-making small group or the disciple-making process, I am contradicting myself. My words may say one thing, but my actions speak another. Imagine the power a church can have when a community of leaders all share agreement and alignment. That kind of church is a force to be reckoned with.

I've been in churches with both mission-minded and self-minded leaders. The difference is astonishing! Like a two-seater bicycle, the mission-minded church moves forward, and the self-minded church stalls. Choose wisely, choose to deny yourself, and follow Christ.

DIG DEEPER

Please read **Proverbs 6:16-19** and write one insight you gleaned from it.

_____
_____
_____

DAY TWELVE

"Great Leaders Model the Mission"

Jesus modeled his mission. He was the perfect model of what he came to be and do. His mission was to make disciples of all nations, so he was the model disciple and the ideal model for making more disciples. Jesus was the best example of what it means to be a disciple and build other disciples. No one was or is a better example to follow than Jesus.

Jesus was the perfect model of living the life we are all called to live. His character and conduct are the ideal examples of the character and conduct we need. Jesus was not asking his disciples to be and do something he wasn't willing to do.

Jesus was the perfect model for leading others to live life. Jesus gave his disciples a great picture of how to help guide someone from untrained to fully trained. What Jesus had done with his disciples was what he expected them to do with others. His words and his deeds were consistent.

Jesus also modeled what it meant to leverage your influence through others. Jesus leveraged his influence through others to help them lead others to live the life they needed to live. By doing this, Jesus gave his disciples a model for leveraging their influence.

If Jesus was the perfect model, we have a long way to go. Perfection isn't the goal for anyone in leadership; progress is the goal. God wants every leader to continue growing and being transformed into the image of Christ. This process is called sanctification, which isn't complete until we enter heaven.

You never graduate from discipleship. You should grow in Christ-like character and conduct for the rest of your life. If you and I met together every week for the rest of our time here on earth, we would always have something to share about how we are doing in our development, or lack thereof, in Christ's likeness. It will be a lifelong process of growth in character and conduct as I search the scriptures, listen to the Holy Spirit, and gain encouragement for others in this transformation. I may not be where I want to be, but hopefully, I am not where I was and not where I will eventually be.

God uses leaders who are becoming more like Christ. The key word is "becoming." Great leaders model the process of becoming like their teacher.

DIG DEEPER

Please read **Luke 6:40** and write one insight you gleaned from it.

_____
_____
_____

DAY THIRTEEN

"Mission Congruent Leaders"

The word "congruent" means to agree or to be accordant. It's taken me over thirty years, but I have realized that one of the essential principles in all leadership is building on mission-congruent leaders. In other words, develop and mobilize leaders that agree and are in accord with the mission you are trying to accomplish. You will never get the right outcome in your mission if it is led by leaders who are not living out the mission. On the other hand, you cannot help but accomplish the mission when you have leaders who are living the mission out. That being true, I think you must seek to have leaders who are mission-congruent.

As I consider this idea of mission-congruent leadership, I know that it begins with me. I can't ask people to be or do something I am not seeking to be and do myself. That's considered inauthentic, and no one likes to follow an inauthentic leader. If you say spending time with God matters, then spend time with God. If you say giving matters, then be a giver. If you say serving is essential, then serve others. If you say sharing Christ matters, then share Christ. If being a person who is faithful, kind, and self-controlled is what you expect from a leader, then seek to be that kind of person. The list continues, but the point is simply this. Be and do what you are asking others to be and do.

I remember hearing a story in seminary about a pastor who regularly preached about tithing. Still, when his giving record was checked, he had not given a dime to that church over many years. It shouldn't be surprising that the church was also in severe financial trouble. I'm sure you've heard the phrase "speed of the leader, speed of the team"? The word implies that the organization will never go farther or faster than the leader is willing to go. That statement has much truth, but it reinforces the need for leaders to live out the mission.

A school system would look for a Superintendent with a particular education level. An army would look for a General with specific military knowledge and experience. A professional sports team would want a coach who has played or coached at a certain level. The church should want spiritually qualified leaders who understand the mission. If we don't go with mission-congruent leaders, we must not be surprised where the church ends up.

DIG DEEPER

Please read **Philippians 2:2** and write one insight you gleaned from it.

_____
_____
_____

DAY FOURTEEN

"Be More Like Jesus"

"Be more like Jesus," could mean many different things if you see it subjectively. If you let scripture define it objectively, it becomes peculiar to say, "Be more like Jesus."

The scripture is very objective when describing what it means to be like Jesus in one's character. The Fruit of the Spirit described in Galatians 5:22-23 is an evident and concise list of character traits you would find in Jesus and should find in his disciples. There may be more ways to describe Christ-like character, but I am sure that love, joy, peace, patience, kindness, goodness, gentleness, faithfulness, and self-control all make the list.

I also believe the Bible is clear and objective when describing Christ-like conduct. The description of the first group of disciples mentioned in Acts 2:41-47 provides us with very accurate behaviors or actions of the disciples that made up the Jerusalem church. These behaviors are all modeled by Jesus in the gospel's accounts. There may be more marks of Christ-like conduct than in Acts 2:41-47, but the marks we see here are all true of Jesus and should be true of his disciples. A disciple of Jesus belongs, grows, serves, worships, manages their resources, shares the messages, and multiplies disciples.

Imagine the difference between defining a leader as "like Jesus" based on objective instead of subjective criteria. There is quite a difference between saying, "I think or feel like they are Christ-like" verses, "Based on scripture, they display Christ-like character traits and marks of conduct." The second option is a lot more trustworthy and concrete when it comes to identifying church leadership.

Before you place a person in church leadership, be sure they are becoming like Jesus. Don't just hope they are! The classic method of selecting church leadership has not gotten the church far. It would make such a massive difference if the church were led by mission-congruent leaders seeking to live like Jesus in their character and conduct. The next page gives you a great chart to identify the right leader.

DIG DEEPER

Please read **John 13:15** and write one insight you gleaned from it.

_____
_____
_____

FULLY TRAINED DISCIPLE

QUESTIONS FOR REFLECTION OR DISCUSSION

The past seven days have helped you learn more about being a Disciple-Making Leader. Please take a few minutes to reflect on the following questions or discuss them with others.

1- What happens when God's church is fuzzy on what our mission is?

2- How can doing "good things" keep us from doing the "best things"? Does this ever happen to you?

3- Share your thoughts on the statement, "When you forget your why, you will lose your way."

4- Why is agreement and alignment so essential to church leadership?

5- In what ways did Jesus model the mission that he has given us?

6- What is a "mission congruent" leader? Why is that important?

7- What do we mean by Christlike character and conduct? Why does it need to be objective rather than subjective?

DAY FIFTEEN

"Great Leaders Execute the Mission"

Great disciple-making leaders do not just model the mission of Jesus; they execute it. In other words, they do what Jesus did! They follow his example in helping untrained seekers become fully trained disciples.

I have been involved in the local church for a long time, and one of the biggest problems in church leadership is having leaders who do not do what Jesus did. Are leaders that do not execute the mission leaders, to begin with? Leaders who do not achieve the mission of Jesus are leaders in name only.

How can someone be called a leader in the church of Jesus Christ who does not even attempt to reach the lost, connect people to the Church, develop disciples, and raise more leaders? If leaders are not executing the mission, what on earth are they doing?

The leaders that Jesus developed did what he did. They executed the same strategy he implemented. That is what makes them great disciple-making leaders. The best example of execution is found in how the Church is described in Acts 2:41-47. This description of church life proves what Jesus' leaders did after his death. The Apostles led the Church in Jerusalem to be a movement of multiplying disciples. In the Jerusalem Church, they were helping untrained seekers become fully trained disciples. They were doing with others what Jesus had done with them. People were coming to faith in Christ, and disciples were being reproduced because the Apostles and their disciples were doing the same things Jesus did. This should still be true of the church today, but I am afraid it isn't.

In the next few days, you will examine how a leader executes the mission. Here is a quick overview of how leaders conduct.

Leaders who execute reach people far from God
Leaders who execute help connect people to God's Church
Leaders who execute train people others to become disciples
Leaders that conduct, develop, and send out more leaders

DIG DEEPER

Please read **John 14:12** and write one insight you gleaned from it.

_____
_____
_____

DAY SIXTEEN

"Leaders Reach Lost People"

Here is a simple concept. If Jesus reached lost people, leaders in his movement should reach lost people! Luke 19:10 makes this so clear you can't miss it. Why did Jesus come according to that verse?

If Jesus came to "seek and save the lost," it makes sense that leaders within his movement are committed to doing the same thing. What's mind-blowing is how many church leaders I know are not reaching the lost or even attempting to do so. How on earth can that be called authentic church leadership?

I believe the church would be putting a deeper dent in the darkness if those who call themselves leaders were executing the same way Jesus did. Remember the speed of the leader, the speed of the team? If church leaders are reaching people far from God, you can rest assured that those who follow them will reach people far from God. People do what they see, not just what they hear.

In Matthew 28:19, Jesus said, "Go therefore and make disciples of all nations..." This part of Christ's Great Commission can best be translated as "as you are going" to make disciples. Jesus is speaking about connecting with and reaching people who do not yet know God. He tells them to prioritize getting people everywhere and leading them to believe in God.

Jesus did the same thing with the disciples a few years before this commissioning. In John 1:39, he said to a couple of his disciples, "Come, and you will see." Jesus was inviting these untrained seekers to come and investigate who he was and what he had to offer them. He was leading them to faith. It was the first step on their journey to becoming the leaders of his movement.

Great disciple-making leaders live a "come and see" lifestyle. They constantly seek opportunities to connect with people far from God and help them come to faith. Reaching lost people is what disciple-making leaders do.

DIG DEEPER

Please read **Luke 10:1-2** and write one insight you gleaned from it.

_____
_____
_____

DAY SEVENTEEN

"Leaders Connect People to Christ's Church"

In The Great Commission (Matthew 28:19), Jesus told his leadership team to make disciples of all nations by "baptizing them in the name of the Father and the Son and the Holy Spirit." Baptizing people was an essential part of making fully trained disciples. The act of baptism identified a person as a member of Christ's mission and his movement. It was a public statement that a person believed and belonged to Christ and his church. To this day, baptism is a step of obedience every believer should take. It does not save a person but shows outwardly the commitments they have made inwardly. A commitment to follow Jesus and to belong to his family.

In Acts 2:41, the Bible says, "So those who received his word were baptized, and there were added about three thousand souls that day." It is obvious that in the Jerusalem church, helping people connect to Christ and His church are both essential parts of the disciple-making process. Once a person comes to faith in Christ, it is vital to help them identify with Christ and a family of believers. Nothing has changed in the last two thousand years. Identifying with Christ and His Church is still an essential step in disciple-making.

Jesus demonstrated this same value when he invited his disciples to come and follow him in John 1:43. By inviting these disciples to follow him, he was asking them to identify with him and with other disciples. He was connecting them to himself and the community. Jesus knew they needed him, but he also knew they would need each other. Especially after they publicly identified as Christ's followers.

In the first century, being a Christ-follower could easily mean that your family wanted to have nothing to do with you. Jesus' followers were often ostracized and rejected by their family and friends. This told that belonging to a spiritual family was essential for their lives. Being connected to a spiritual family was not optional. No one was "church shopping" in Jerusalem.

Great disciple-making leaders help people connect to God's church. They live a lifestyle of assisting people to participate in baptism and belonging to a church family. Connecting people is what they do.

DIG DEEPER

Please read **Acts 8:36-38** and write one insight you gleaned from it.

_____
_____
_____

DAY EIGHTEEN

"Leaders Train More Disciples"

Jesus made leaders who execute the mission by reminding them that leading means teaching or training. He told his leaders to make disciples of all nations by baptizing them and "teaching them to observe all that I have commanded you" (Matthew 28:20).

The church does not need leaders sitting in rooms with business agendas and voting on things. That is necessary, but the church also needs leaders that do the mission. The church needs leaders who train and teach other disciples, making leaders like Jesus did. The church needs leaders who lead others to observe what Jesus has commanded.

I know some will disagree with this statement, but a church leader who is not making disciples does not need to be in leadership. Sometimes, a leader may not be engaged in the disciple-making process, but overall, every leader should live a lifestyle of disciple-making. I do not believe Jesus saw it any other way. Jesus saw his leadership team as a disciple-making team.

The apostles knew how to train and teach leaders by replicating what Jesus had done with them. He had given them a model for how to train others. He had instructed them, and now they were ready to teach others. They would, in turn, train others who could do the same thing and pass down what being a disciple meant to even more people. This ripple effect would eventually impact all nations!

Mark 3:14 shows us clearly the approach that Jesus used. "And he appointed twelve (whom he also named apostles) so that they might be with him and he might send them out to preach."

Jesus spent time training his disciples to send them out to make more disciples. They did the same thing he did.

The church today needs leaders who are disciple-makers. The church needs leaders to train others to be fully trained disciples by being with them and sending them out. Teaching and training others to observe Christ's commands should be standard operating procedures for all church leaders. Leaders should live a lifestyle of executing the mission by training more disciples. Teaching more disciples is what leaders do.

DIG DEEPER

Please read **Deuteronomy 31:7-8** and write one insight you gleaned from it.

_____
_____
_____

DAY NINETEEN

"Leaders Develop and Launch More Leaders"

A few years ago, I invited a handful of men to meet with me every week for a discipleship group. Every week, we held each other accountable, studied the life of Christ together, and encouraged and prayed for each other. When they were ready, I pressed some men to step up and start new groups they would lead. A few more years have passed, and now those guys have completed training the guys in their groups and are ready to raise and send out more leaders. That is an example of how leaders develop and launch more leaders.

What I did with a small group of men is similar to what Jesus did with a handful over two thousand years ago. Jesus spent three years developing disciples who would become his movement's leaders. He launched them out, and they began discipling and raising other leaders in the New Testament Church. The priority of leaders developing and launching more leaders has stayed the same for over two thousand years. The plan still works if we work it.

In all my years as a Christian, I know very few people who have intentionally developed and launched more leaders. I think that has a great deal to do with the state of the church today. Most of the leaders I know ended up in leadership unintentionally and in some ways by accident. There is a vast difference between "good old boy" and strategic and intentional leadership development. The latter is preferred if we want a disciple-making church and a movement of multiplying disciples.

Great leaders execute the mission by disciplining people and appointing them to leadership assignments. Raising and sending leaders out is a lifestyle of great leaders committed to executing Jesus's process.

When you look at the fruit of your life, how many leaders are making disciples in the world because you invested in them and helped them become fully trained disciples who are now leaders? If the answer to that question is none, then it is time to get busy making disciples who become disciple-making leaders.

DIG DEEPER

Please read **Exodus 18:25** and write one insight you gleaned from it.

_____
_____
_____

DAY TWENTY

"Great Leaders Multiply the Mission"

Here is a huge question. Are you making leaders by addition or multiplication? Let's be honest: if leaders are developing and raising new leaders, they are likely doing it through addition, not multiplication. The difference is vitally important. When you create and launch a leader, that's an addition. When you develop and launch a leader that develops and launches additional leaders, that is multiplication.

I believe Jesus would say that a leader leading by multiplying disciples is a leader living a "much fruit" life. In John 15:8, Jesus says, "By this, my Father is glorified, that you may bear much fruit and so prove to be my disciples." In John fifteen, Jesus talks about several levels of fruit-bearing. He talks about "no fruit," "some fruit," "more fruit," and "much fruit." The "much fruit" life is the life that reproduces exponentially and creates a legacy of leaders that multiply more disciples. A leader who develops multiple generations of leaders is one of the marks of outstanding leadership.

Let's cut to the chase. Take a minute and write down the names of leaders that you have personally developed and launched that have developed and launched more leaders.

_____

_____

_____

Paul is an excellent example of a leader that multiplies the mission. In 2 Timothy 2:2, Paul tells his disciples, "What you have heard from me in the presence of many witnesses entrusted to faithful men who will be able to teach others also." In this passage, Paul is living a much fruitful life. He has discipled Timothy, who invests in faithful men who can teach others also. This passage demonstrates three generations of disciples. It shows us how leaders multiply their vision through others.

How many generations of disciples and leaders can you identify from your life? Regardless of your answer, you want to become a leader that multiplies. You want to live a "much fruit" life and be known for living a lifestyle of multiplication.

DIG DEEPER

Please read **Psalm 78:4** and write one insight you gleaned from it.

_____
_____
_____

DAY TWENTY-ONE

"Look for a Timothy"

To be a leader that multiplies the mission, you must look for a Timothy. A Timothy is that person or group of people with whom you will begin the disciple-making process. For Jesus, it was the original twelve. Paul started with a disciple named Timothy, who found faithful men he could invest in and turn around and invest in others. Remember, you will only create a disciple-making movement once you start with at least one person.

Timothy had proven himself to Paul. Paul knew that Timothy was coachable and reliable. He knew he was as trustworthy and faithful as the guys he encouraged Timothy to find. The kind of person Paul was instructing Timothy to select was the same kind of person Paul set when he chose Timothy. These faithful men were Timothy's. They were trustworthy, reliable, and able to teach others. When you find the right person, you dramatically raise the percentage of successful multiplication. You increase the odds tremendously when you invest your time in someone willing to show up, work hard, and learn from others.

On the other hand, you will not get very far when you try to invest in people who don't show up, don't put forth much effort, and already know it all.

Acts 4:13 tells us that Peter and John "were uneducated, common men." This one verse tells us a great deal about the kind of men Jesus invested his life in. Jesus made disciples out of simple fishermen. They were not highly educated, highly gifted, or entrepreneurs. However, Jesus could depend on them, and he could teach them. The disciples became great leaders not because of their accomplishments but because of their willingness to be used.

Leaders who multiply the mission must select the type of person who will take and reproduce what they have learned. Not everyone will breed and multiply. Finding people with the necessary intangibles to keep the process going would be best. Always look for someone who has demonstrated this potential in some way before committing to invest in them. Test them out before inviting them to join you. Remember, the best indicator of future success is always past performance.

DIG DEEPER

Please read **2 Kings 2:15** and write one insight you gleaned from it.

_____
_____
_____

QUESTIONS FOR REFLECTION OR DISCUSSION

The past seven days have helped you learn more about being a Disciple-Making Leader. Please take a few minutes to reflect on the following questions or discuss them with others.

1- Why would we say that great leaders execute the mission? Why is that important?

2- Why must leaders "reaching people" be a part of their lifestyle?

3- Do you think most leaders see their role as helping people take the step of baptism and connect to the church? Why or why not?

4- How important is it for leaders to teach and train others? How common is that in most churches?

5- How do you think most churches prioritize leadership development and recruitment? How does that impact the movement of Christ?

6- How did Paul live a "much fruit" life? Why is that important for leaders?

7- What should you look for in a person you want to disciple?

DAY TWENTY-TWO

"Priorities or Pressure"

Everyone knows the key to winning a relay race is the exchange. Its successful passing of the baton enables a relay team to win. A team can be faster than another, but if they drop the baton, they will probably lose. Passing that baton from one runner to another to another is the name of the game in winning relay races.

Passing the baton is also the name of the game in multiplying disciples. If the exchange is not made and the baton is dropped in making disciples, there is a good chance that reproduction won't happen.

Jesus was successful in passing the baton. Paul was successful in making the exchange to Timothy. Timothy was successful in passing the baton to trustworthy and faithful men. Loyal and faithful men were able to exchange with other men who were also able to teach others. You and I know Christ today and are experiencing abundant life because many people have successfully paid the baton for thousands of years.

The message of Jesus and the methods of Jesus are the baton we need to pass on to others. If we don't pass down the message, people miss Jesus's good news and salvation. If we don't pass down the methods of Jesus, people miss out on how to live like Jesus and help others learn how to live like Jesus. The message and methods are the mission!

Jesus has told us to make disciples of all nations that are fully trained and look like their teachers. That means they have come to faith in Christ, are following Christ, and becoming more like Christ.

When great leaders multiply the mission and don't try to teach everything a disciple could know, they teach everything a disciple needs to know. Those are two very different things. Jesus never attempted to teach his disciples every doctrinal issue and every biblical truth. Jesus set out to make disciples that could make more disciples. Jesus knew that if he made disciples who looked like him, they would continue to grow and learn more independently. He knew they would become lifelong learners.

Once you find your Timothy's, focus on giving them the message of Christ and the methods of Christ. Teach them how to be a disciple and build more disciples, and that will ensure the baton gets passed.

DIG DEEPER

Please read **Acts 6:3** and write one insight you gleaned from it.

_____
_____
_____

DAY TWENTY-THREE

"Teach Them How to Fish"

I'm sure you've heard this saying. "You can catch fish for a man or teach a man how to catch fish." What a great statement, and maybe no greater way to describe the role of a leader that multiplies.

My dad taught me how to fish for fish. He showed me how to put bait on a hook, cast a line in the right place, and reel in the fish when hooked. After watching him do it, he helped me do the same thing, and I did it all alone. Years later, I found myself doing the same thing with my sons. I was taught how to catch fish on my own, and then I taught others how to catch fish on their own.

In Matthew 4:19, Jesus said, "Follow me, and I will make you fishers of men." Jesus wants to have disciples who learn from him by being with him, and then he wants to send those disciples out to teach more men how to follow him and then reach even more men.

This week, I talked with a leader who recently took a group of men through a two-year discipleship process. They have been meeting weekly for two years to be trained to go out and disciple more men. This leader tells me that his group has decided to study another Christian resource. Using another resource is okay, but we have a goal in mind for why groups like his should use our resource. The goal was to train his group members to go out and train more people.

I recently heard a great quote like this, "There is no success without a successor." Jesus' disciples did not study another resource or curriculum at the end of three years. The time I had come to expand, reach, and teach more people. The time had come to go fishing!

Jesus' disciple-making ministry was only successful because he equipped his twelve disciples to go out and share the mission with others. The Christian movement would have ceased with the disciples if they had only remained a small group. Great disciple-making leaders multiply more disciples.

DIG DEEPER

Please read **1 Corinthians 11:1** and write one insight you gleaned from it.

_____
_____
_____

DAY TWENTY-FOUR

"Great Leaders Protect the Mission"

Great leaders defend and protect the mission of Christ. They do not sit by and watch people attack it and criticize it. They keep their dukes up and fight for unity and harmony within the movement of Christ. They do everything they can to protect and defend the bride of Christ.

Imagine a leader in our nation's military not protecting the mission that our troops are fighting for. Imagine a business leader creating disunity within a company or corporation that demoralizes employees. Think about an athletic leader on a team who questions the coaches and criticizes their decisions. Think of a church with leaders spewing critical and negative things about the pastor or other church leaders. Every example mentioned above happens when leaders forget that part of their job is to protect the mission.

It pains me to say this, but I have been in one too many churches that have had conflict or division that has derailed the mission. If I didn't know better, it almost seemed Satan liked it that way. Yes, I am being very sarcastic. The truth is Satan is using every resource at his disposal to stop the mission of Christ from advancing. He knows the power of multiplication and will do everything he can to keep it from occurring.

One of the best ways to attack the church's mission is from within. Sometimes, an attack from the outside makes devotion to the mission stronger. Attack, from the inside, however, is the trump card for the enemy. Satan knows that if he can get leaders focused on themselves, it will keep them from focusing on what matters: the mission.

In Mark 3:25, Jesus says, "And if a house is divided against itself, that house will not be able to stand." That is straightforward and clearly articulates one of Satan's most excellent strategies against the mission. Divide its leaders.

At some point, everyone must understand that the mission is more important than personal preferences. Please understand that if something is unbiblical, unethical, immoral, or illegal, that is not a personal preference. That is wrong, and it must be dealt with. On the other hand, personality differences and political agendas must be dealt with and resolved for the sake of the mission. That requires leaders who fight for and protect the mission.

DIG DEEPER

Please read **Romans 16:17-18** and write one insight you gleaned from it.

_____
_____
_____

DAY TWENTY-FIVE

"When Conflict Comes"

People are broken, and churches are made up of broken people. That means churches are broken, and problems and conflicts will occur. The key is dealing with issues and conflicts quickly and decisively so that it does not impair mission progress. Satan loves to stir up conflict to keep God's people from accomplishing the mission. I can't tell you how many times I've seen good-hearted, well-meaning people be at odds with each other over things that don't matter. That seems to be Satan's specialty.

The church needs leaders that don't allow disunity and conflict to fester. The church needs leaders who sniff out every spark of dissension and squelch it. The church needs leaders who won't allow division and conflict to exist and will do everything they can to handle it correctly.

In Acts 15:39, there is an excellent example of how the enemy tries to stop the mission through disunity. The Bible says, "And there arose a sharp disagreement so that they separated. Barnabas took Mark and sailed away to Cyprus, but Paul chose Silas and departed..." Even Paul was attacked by the enemy, and Satan tried using conflict and disagreement to stop the spread of the gospel.

Interestingly, in Philippians 4:2, Paul encourages two women to put their disagreements behind them and work together for the cause of Christ. Paul says, "I entreat Euodia and I entreat Syntyche to agree in the Lord." Paul was a leader who understood the importance of unity and working together for the mission. He also knew that sometimes we must agree to disagree when the conflict is too great.

I've heard it said that every Christian is a two-bucket Christian. We have a bucket of gas and water; the one we throw when we see a spark of division is up to us. That's such a powerful and true statement. I've been part of a church that split wide open because someone threw gas on a tiny spark of division that led to a blaze that was out of control. That church is where I was baptized; it does not exist today. I would say the mission was derailed. We need church leaders who are committed to protecting the mission.

DIG DEEPER

Please read **Romans 12:18** and write one insight you gleaned from it.

_____
_____
_____

DAY TWENTY-SIX

"You Can't Rock A Boat You're Rowing"

I love the old saying, "You can't rock the boat if you are rowing it!" I wish I knew who said that. It was probably a pastor trying to get his church leaders focused on making a disciple-making movement.

It doesn't take much to realize that people not rowing, i.e., doing the mission, can easily get caught up in rocking the boat. It is easy to find all that is not working and see all the negative things when you are not busy making things happen. On the other hand, it is tough to rock the boat and create disunity when you are working hard to row the boat so it will move forward in fulfilling the mission.

When a person sits and soaks, it is only a matter of time till they sour. The person who is active and working hard on the mission differs from the person who complains about everything. The person who complains is usually not carrying their weight and doing their part of the mission.

I never mind hearing constructive criticism; I wouldn't say I like hearing it from people who are not doing anything. I always tell people you can say anything you want if you are in the foxhole with me. If, on the other hand, you are not being fired on and fighting the battle, you have waived your right to criticize. I'm not interested in hearing negativity from people staying safely behind the battle line. However, I welcome all suggestions from people standing beside me in the battle.

I cannot emphasize enough the importance of having church leaders that protect the mission and unity of the church. Again, I do not suggest unity at "all costs." Sometimes, when sin is involved, disunity is necessary. When it is not a sin issue, unity is always the plan.

Ask yourself why if you are a leader who can't protect the mission. If it is the proper mission, The Great Commission, why can't you get behind it? You do not want to be the leader known for bucking the mission of God's church. You do not wish to have a division on your resume! Great leaders protect God's mission for the church of Jesus Christ.

DIG DEEPER

Please read **Psalm 133:1** and write one insight you gleaned from it.

_____
_____
_____

DAY TWENTY-SEVEN

"Great Leaders Finish the Mission"

Lots of people start things, but only a few finish them. Only a few people see things to the end. Only a handful of people accomplish the mission they have been given. Be one of those people. Be a leader that finishes the mission Jesus gave you.

Jesus finished the mission he was given. In John 17:4, Jesus is praying and says to his father, "I glorified you on earth, having accomplished the work that you gave me to do." Jesus is near the end of his life, and he is telling his father that he has finished his mission. If that was true of Jesus, how much more do we need that to be true of us? Every leader needs to be able to say at the end of their life that they have accomplished the work God gave them to do.

The work Jesus refers to in John 17 differs from the one he would accomplish on the cross. On the cross, Jesus said, "It is finished" because he made redemption possible for all who placed their faith in him. In John 17:4, Jesus is referring to the work of starting a multiplying movement of disciples. At this point, Jesus was sure his disciples would go out and make more disciples. He had trained and tested them and knew they would continue his mission.

Jesus is not expecting us to make redemption possible. He is expecting us to continue multiplying messengers of redemption. Those messengers are called disciples!

The big question is this. How are you doing at continuing the mission of making disciples? What would happen if Christ's whole movement and mission rested with you? If you can't say you are investing in disciples who will go out and reproduce more disciples, then you are not finishing the work Jesus gave you.

It is good to finish a task; it is even better to complete the right task. There are several things I want to end well. I want to spend my marriage well. I want to finish being a father. I want to finish being a pastor well. I want to finish many things well, but I want to complete the mission of "making disciples of all nations" well. I do not want to stand before God someday and tell him I did everything well except the mission. May we all finish the mission well.

DIG DEEPER

Please read **2 Corinthians 4:16-18** and write one insight you gleaned from it.

_____
_____
_____

DAY TWENTY-EIGHT

"Obey"

The key to finishing well can be summed up in one word: obedience. We will complete the mission well if we do what Jesus told us. If we make excuses, get distracted, and give up, we should not be surprised if we don't finish the mission.

It has been said that the "best offense is a good defense." I would suggest you be on the lookout for "obedience busters." The enemy will throw dozens of things at you to try and keep you from being obedient to the very end. In Luke 9:57-62 the obedience busters are on full display. After handling several objections to following him, Jesus said, "No one who puts his hand to the plow and looks back is fit for the kingdom of God." Jesus is simply saying, finish the mission.

I am amazed at how many people make excuses for not doing their part in making disciples of all nations. At some point, the excuses fade, and you have either been a part of the mission of making disciples or haven't. It is that simple. You cannot change the mission. You cannot pretend Jesus didn't give it. You cannot do away with it. So, therefore, you either do it or you don't.

I have a friend who says, "Christ's last command should be our priority." I agree that anything that is a priority will bring obedience.

Doing your part in the mission of Jesus means one of two things- either being a disciple or building more disciples. If you still need to be qualified to build disciples, then be in the process of becoming a fully trained disciple. If you are a fully trained disciple, make more disciples.

A guy once told me that "multiplying disciples just doesn't work." I'm afraid I have to disagree. He didn't become a Christian because multiplication does not work. How can he explain his faith apart from a group of men on a mountainside in Galilee being obedient to Jesus' last command? If the original disciples had not made more disciples, this guy would never have heard of Jesus, and he would have spent the rest of eternity separated from God in a place called hell.

If this guy does not obey Christ's last command today, then the next generation of people might not hear about Christ. There is so much at stake in our obedience. Let's not let the next generation miss knowing what it means to be a disciple because of our disobedience.

DIG DEEPER

Please read **2 Timothy 2:4-6** and write one insight you gleaned from it.

_____
_____
_____

DAY TWENTY-NINE

"Keep Your Eye on the Prize"

I ran track in high school and quickly learned how important the finish line is. The goal of every race I ran was always the same: make it to the finish line. The goal was never to have great form. Make a great picture. Wear a clean uniform, or play it safe not to get hurt. The goal was to finish before anyone else, if possible.

Being a leader is like running a track. It is challenging, and sometimes you feel like giving up. That's why keeping your eyes on the prize is always essential. That means keeping your eyes on the finish line. The goal of every leader should be to finish and finish well. The goal of every leader should be to hear the words of Jesus from Matthew 25:21, "Well done, good and faithful servant. You have been faithful over little; I will set you over much. Enter into the joy of your master."

Jesus said these words regarding a servant who had received five talents and brought his master five more. He reproduced his resources. He invested well and brought back more than he started with.

This story is an excellent picture of what it means to be a disciple-making leader. Your goal as a disciple-making leader is to bring back to God more disciples than you started with. The prize, the finish line, is to multiply more disciples for the Kingdom of God.

As we've seen, Paul is one of Scripture's most outstanding examples of a disciple-making leader. He started persecuting disciples, became one, and then made more of them. That is excellent disciple-making leadership. In 2 Timothy 4:7, Paul is nearing the end of his life, and here is what he says about his life. "I have fought the good fight, I have finished the race, I have kept the faith."

I am confident that Paul will hear the Lord say, "Well done, good and faithful servant. You have been faithful over little; I will set you over much. Enter into the joy of your master." Paul finished, and he finished well. He didn't just stumble over the finish line. He won the prize. He left behind a legacy of disciples who are still making disciples. You may have even come for the disciple-making lineage of Paul. The real question is, who will go from yours?

DIG DEEPER

Please read **1 Corinthians 9:24-27** and write one insight you gleaned from it.

_____
_____
_____

DAY TWENTY-THIRTY

"What Kind of Leader Are You?"

The whole point of this little book is to illustrate what a great disciple-making leader looks like. This is not a book about disciple-making pastors or staff members. This book encourages the ordinary, uneducated man or woman in the typical church who seeks to obey Jesus and fulfill the mission of making disciples. It is for the volunteer, lay leader (for lack of a better term) who is doing their best to honor God by making disciples who make more disciples. God wants to use this group of men and women to change the world. It is not just the seminary trained but the ordinary person in the pew that God intends to use for the most significant impact.

So the big question as we bring this resource to an end is, what kind of leader are you? Are you the kind of disciple-making leader described in this book's pages? Are you a leader who knows the mission, models the mission, executes the mission, multiplies the mission, protects the mission, and finishes the mission, or are you still in the process? If you stood before the Lord, would you hear him say, "Well done, good and faithful servant"?

I hope and pray you are in a church with a disciple-making focus. If not, you still want to obey the last command of Jesus. If you do so, maybe your church will notice the fruit of your life and investigate how to become a disciple-making church. Until then, you will still want to apply the principles you have discovered in this book. Remember, Jesus did not say, "Make disciples if your church is making them" or "If your pastor is making them." He expects you to make them regardless of who is and who isn't making them. Be the kind of leader Jesus is honored by and who stays true to the mission. Be the leader that makes Christ's last command your priority.

I often say, "Jesus started the church the way he wanted it, and now he wants it the way he started it." I could also add, "Jesus created you the way he wanted you, and now he wants you the way he created you." Jesus created you to be a disciple and build more disciples. It's time to make that the story and legacy of your life. Become a great disciple-making leader!

DIG DEEPER

Please read **1 John 2:6** and write one insight you gleaned from it.

_____
_____
_____

QUESTIONS FOR REFLECTION OR DISCUSSION

The past seven days have helped you learn more about being a Disciple-Making Leader. Please take a few minutes to reflect on the following questions or discuss them with others.

1- Share a practical example of how someone has taught you to do something and you have taught someone else to do the same thing.

2- Do you have a personal example of how 2 Timothy 2:2 has been fleshed out today?

3- Why and how does Satan attack the mission of making disciples?

4- What is the best way to avoid conflict and negativity? How can a person promote unity?

5- What does it mean that Jesus finished the mission?

6- What can become obstacles to finishing, and how can we overcome them?

7- How would you evaluate yourself based on the six priorities of a disciple-making leader?

WHAT IS YOUR NEXT STEP?

Imagine taking all your disciple-making leaders through an online training based on the six priorities of a Disciple-Making Leader you just discovered. Here is how our process works:

Step One: A pastor, discipleship pastor, or another key leader joins a Disciple-Making Leader online equipping group led by a trainer from Impact Discipleship Ministries. Over seven weeks, those leaders will be trained to lead disciple-making leaders within your church.

Step Two: Upon completing the Disciple-Making Leader group, your pastor, discipleship pastor, or key leader will be equipped to use that training process in your church. You can then have your other leaders go through our training, or you can develop a leadership process based on the training you've received for your leaders.

Step Three: Once your church begins the Disciple-Making Leader training, you might consider using the Impact curriculum and working through the consultation process to develop a "MAP" (Ministry Action Plan) for your church. Impact Discipleship Ministries is here to help you learn how to be and build disciples of Christ.

Contact us and take your next step at impactdisciples.com.

ABOUT THE AUTHOR:
KEN ADAMS

Adams was called as the first pastor of Crossroads Church, Newnan in June 1989. He has a passion for being a disciple of Christ and pouring his life into others who desire to "walk as Jesus walked." Adams grew up in Stone Mountain, GA, and graduated from Southwestern Theological Seminary with a Master of Divinity.

After searching the market and not finding adequate disciple-making resources to help achieve the spiritual growth goals of Crossroads, Adams began writing his own curriculum. His resources were so successful in achieving Crossroad's goals that he decided to make them available to other churches. Impact Discipleship Ministries, Inc. was founded for that purpose in 2002.

Today, churches all over the world use Impact's curriculum. Adams continues to lead training seminars on the Disciple-Making Church strategy, and continues to develop new resources to help churches and individuals develop fully trained disciples of Jesus Christ.

DISCIPLE-MAKING CHURCH
SEMINARS

What if **one year** of changing your disciple-making strategy meant exponential growth for your small groups?

Impact is here to help you actualize your vision of multiplying disciples of Jesus Christ. Fully trained disciples will impact the entire world. Their education and direction starts with your small groups.

Let us teach you how simple a good disciple-making strategy can really be! We will help you identify your goals and develop a strategy based on Christ's model to multiply disciples in your church.

WHAT YOU LEARN

> Define the disciple-making mission of the Church
> Explore the model Jesus gave to make disciples
> Learn the method Jesus used to multiply disciples

THE MAKING OF A DISCIPLE-MAKING PASTOR

ONLINE EQUIPPING GROUPS

Are you passionate about leading your church to multiply disciples, but do not feel equipped to accomplish that mission?

In our equipping groups, you will study the six priorities of Disciple-Making Pastors and learn how to apply those priorities practically in your leadership. You will learn these principles alongside other Disciple-Making Pastors pursuing the mission of Jesus in your equipping group.

Go to our website today and reserve your spot!

LEARN HOW TO:

- Lead Toward the Mission
- Lead Yourself
- Lead the Organization
- Lead Leaders
- Lead with a Plan
- Lead Well

 (678) 854-9322 | info@impactdisciples.com

LEARN MORE

We offer other great book studies, free resources, blogs, podcasts, and more available at *impactdisciples.com*.

   @ImpactDiscipleship

   @ImpactDisciples

Made in the USA
Columbia, SC
18 November 2024

46758056R00043